FORT WORTH PUBLIC LIBRARY
W9-AVM-769

The Pilgrims' Thanksgiving from A to Z

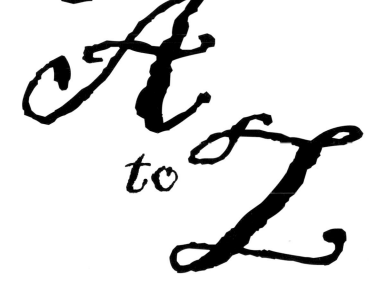

The Pilgrims' Thanksgiving from A to Z

By Laura Crawford

Illustrated by Judith Hierstein

PELICAN PUBLISHING COMPANY

GRETNA 2005

FORT WORTH PUBLIC LIBRARY

Text copyright © 2005
By Laura Crawford

Illustrations copyright © 2005
By Judith Hierstein
All rights reserved

*The word "Pelican" and the depiction of a pelican are trademarks
of Pelican Publishing Company, Inc., and are registered in the
U.S. Patent and Trademark Office.*

Library of Congress Cataloging-in-Publication Data

Crawford, Laura
  The Pilgrims' Thanksgiving from A to Z / by Laura Crawford ; illustrated
by Judith Hierstein.
    p. cm.
  Summary: This alphabet book follows the voyage of the Pilgrims from
England to the New World and their first Thanksgiving.
  ISBN-13: 978-1-58980-238-4 (pbk.)
  1. Thanksgiving Day—Juvenile Literature. [1. Pilgrims (New Plymouth
Colony) 2. Thanksgiving Day. 3. Alphabet.] I. Hierstein, Judy, ill. II. Title.

GT4975.C675 2004
394.2649—dc22

                                                                    2004003453

Printed in Singapore
Published by Pelican Publishing Company, Inc.
1000 Burmaster Street, Gretna, Louisiana 70053

A is for Atlantic Ocean

The Pilgrims sailed across the cold and stormy Atlantic Ocean on September 6, 1620. Their voyage from England to Massachusetts lasted sixty-five days. The Pilgrims were searching for a home where they could be free to make their own religious choices.

B is for boat

The Pilgrims' three-masted ship, the *Mayflower,* was small, only about ninety feet long. The *Mayflower* had been a cargo ship and was not meant to carry passengers. The Pilgrims packed the ship with chests, a cradle, and supplies for their new homes. They lived on the *Mayflower* until their houses were built.

C is for clothing

Pilgrims wore brightly colored clothing, not black clothes with buckles. Women and girls wore skirts and waistcoats or full-length dresses. Men dressed in sleeveless cloaks. Boys wore dresses, called coats, until the age of six.

D is for danger

Stormy weather made the winter voyage dangerous. One passenger was thrown overboard. Clinging to the topsail of the ship, he was dipped into the icy ocean until sailors fished him out with a boat hook. Seasick and scared, the Pilgrims wanted to return home.

E *is for English settlers*

One hundred and two Pilgrims sailed from England to Massachussetts aboard the *Mayflower*. Most parents brought their entire family, but some left children in England. Pilgrim men left jobs as barrel makers, shopkeepers, leather makers, and tailors. There was also one doctor.

F is for freedom

The Pilgrims wanted to start a new life away from England. Some searched for a home where they could freely practice their religion. Others left England to find a land with more jobs. Everyone worked together to build a new country where they had the freedom to live and worship as they chose.

G is for Governor John Carver

John Carver, a brave man with a positive attitude, was the first Pilgrim governor. In 1620 he supported the Mayflower Compact, which established laws for the Pilgrims to follow in their new home. Carver also made a peace treaty with Chief Massasoit. The treaty was an agreement between the Indians and the Pilgrims that prevented them from attacking or stealing from one another.

 **H** *is for hardship*

The Pilgrims did not have much medicine or food. Many became sick as they built their homes in freezing weather. By springtime almost half of them had died of pneumonia or scurvy. The remaining Pilgrims were weak and sad, but despite these hardships, they worked hard to build a settlement.

I is for Indian friends

When the Pilgrims arrived in Massachusetts, the Indians ran away once they saw the new settlers. One day Samoset, a tall Indian man, walked into the settlement and shocked the Pilgrims by saying, "Welcome, Englishmen." Later he introduced the Pilgrims to Chief Massasoit and Squanto, who also became friends with the Pilgrims.

J is for jobs

The main jobs of Pilgrim women were to cook, sew, and raise the children. Men farmed and built homes. Children helped to prepare meals, feed the animals, and clean the settlement.

K is for kitchen

Each house had a small kitchen. Pilgrims ate with knives, spoons, and their fingers. They shared plates. Women baked a weekly supply of bread in a large community oven.

L is for leader

William Bradford was one of the original Pilgrim leaders and the second governor. He was reelected thirty times. Bradford's book, *Of Plymouth Plantation,* was published two hundred years after his death, and it continues to be an important source of information about the Pilgrims.

M is for Miles Standish

Miles Standish was an English soldier who trained the Pilgrims to defend themselves. It is said that Standish stood only five feet two inches tall and had red hair and a temper. He learned the Indian language and was able to communicate with the Pilgrims' Indian friends.

Miles Standish

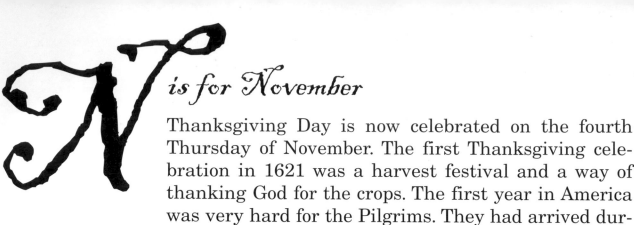

N is for November

Thanksgiving Day is now celebrated on the fourth Thursday of November. The first Thanksgiving celebration in 1621 was a harvest festival and a way of thanking God for the crops. The first year in America was very hard for the Pilgrims. They had arrived during the winter and worked throughout the spring and summer. By autumn they had successfully built their new home and were ready to celebrate.

O is for Oceanus Hopkins

Oceanus Hopkins was born to Elizabeth Hopkins in 1620 on the journey to the New World. Another baby named Peregrine (which means Pilgrim) White was the first child born after the Pilgrims settled in New England.

P is for Plymouth Plantation

Plymouth is called America's Hometown, and it lies on the rocky shore of Massachusetts. The Pilgrims originally called their new settlement Plymouth Plantation. Homes with thatched roofs lined a dirt road through the middle of their town. The Pilgrims also built the Meeting House and used it for religious services and important gatherings.

Q is for quahog

Quahogs are purple clams found along the Atlantic coast. They bury themselves deep in sand or mud, so they have to be dug up. Squanto used quahog shells as tools for planting, and he taught the Pilgrims that they could use the quahogs not only as tools but also as food. The Pilgrims, however only ate clams, lobsters, and oysters when they had nothing else to eat.

R is for Plymouth Rock

Plymouth Rock lies near the area where the Pilgrims are believed to have first arrived in the New World. It is not clear if the Pilgrims really set foot on Plymouth Rock. Today one-third of the original rock is encased for tourists to see.

S is for Squanto

Squanto changed the lives of the Pilgrims by teaching them that fish, especially alewives, could be used as fertilizer. When the seeds were buried with fish, crops grew better. Squanto became friends with the Pilgrims and lived the rest of his life with them.

T is for turkey

Turkey is a traditional part of the Thanksgiving meal, but no one knows if turkey was eaten at the first Thanksgiving. In *Of Plymouth Plantation*, Governor Bradford writes that turkeys were in the area, but he does not say if they were eaten.

U *is for unity*

Grateful for the harvest and Indian help, the Pilgrims organized a three-day Thanksgiving celebration. The huge feast included cornbread, duck, goose, venison, eel, shellfish, and wild plums. Women cooked over outdoor fires. Chief Massasoit and about ninety Indians brought deer to share with the fifty-two Pilgrims.

V is for vegetables

With the Indians' help, the Pilgrims improved their crops. They planted corn, pumpkins, beans, peas, carrots, onions, and turnips. These vegetables helped the Pilgrims grow strong and healthy.

W is for Wampanoag tribe

The Wampanoag tribe lived in about thirty villages in what is now Rhode Island and Massachusetts. The tribe taught the Pilgrims to fish, hunt, gather, and grow their own food. The Pilgrims would not have survived without the help of these Indians.

X is in ax

Pilgrims needed tools to build homes and plant crops. They brought axes, hammers, and nails from England. They used hoes, shovels, and rakes to plant seeds.

Y is for Yellow Feather

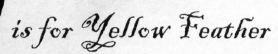

"Yellow Feather" and "Great Chief" were Chief Massasoit's nicknames. His peace treaty with Governor Carver made sure the Pilgrims and Indians worked together. This treaty lasted all of his life.

Z *is in maize*

Maize, or corn, may have saved the Pilgrims from starving. Indians taught the Pilgrims to grow corn that had yellow, red, blue, and black kernels. Indians also introduced dishes such as corn pudding, fried corn cakes, cornbread, and corn soup.